THE BEST DRIVERS OF
FORMULA ONE

BY CORBU STATHES

SportsZone

An Imprint of Abdo Publishing
abdobooks.com

abdobooks.com

Published by Abdo Publishing, a division of ABDO, PO Box 398166, Minneapolis, Minnesota 55439. Copyright © 2024 by Abdo Consulting Group, Inc. International copyrights reserved in all countries. No part of this book may be reproduced in any form without written permission from the publisher. SportsZone™ is a trademark and logo of Abdo Publishing.

Printed in the United States of America, North Mankato, Minnesota.
052023
092023

Cover Photo: Mario Renzi/Formula 1/Getty Images
Interior Photos: Bryn Lennon/Formula 1/Getty Images, 4; Hoch Zwei/Picture-Alliance/DPA/AP Images, 6, 15, 24; Luca Bruno/AP Images, 9; Eugene Hoshiko/AP Images, 11; Sem Van der Wal/ANP/Getty Images Sport/Getty Images, 12; Victor R. Caivano/AP Images, 16; Eric Gaillard/Pool Reuters/AP Images, 19; Gongora/NurPhoto/Getty Images, 21; Remko de Waal/ANP/Getty Images Sport/Getty Images, 22; Alex Pantling/Formula 1/Getty Images, 26; Peter Fox/Getty Images Sport/Getty Images, 28; Joe Portlock/Formula 1/Formula Motorsport Limited/Getty Images, 29

Editor: Charlie Beattie
Series Designer: Michael J. Williams

Library of Congress Control Number: 2022949088

Publisher's Cataloging-in-Publication Data

Names: Stathes, Corbu, author.
Title: The best drivers of formula one / by Corbu Stathes
Description: Minneapolis, Minnesota: Abdo Publishing Company, 2024 | Series: Focus on formula one | Includes online resources and index.
Identifiers: ISBN 9781098290726 (lib. bdg.) | ISBN 9781098276904 (ebook)
Subjects: LCSH: Formula One automobiles--Juvenile literature. | Automobile racing drivers--Juvenile literature. | Racers (Persons)--Juvenile literature.
Classification: DDC 796.72--dc23

TABLE OF
CONTENTS

Sir Lewis Hamilton holds up the Union Jack flag after winning the 2021 British Grand Prix.

CHAPTER ONE

THE UNITED KINGDOM

Confidence, a quick wit, and courage are all qualities drivers need to thrive at the top level of open-wheel racing. Formula One drivers push their cars to speeds above 220 miles per hour (354 km/h). They must handle the twists and turns of Grand Prix tracks while surrounded by rival drivers trying to overtake them. And they do it all with a worldwide audience watching. These are some of the best drivers the world has to offer.

The United Kingdom has a long tradition of Grand Prix racing. The first modern British Grand

Hamilton won his seventh championship in 2020.

Prix was run in 1948. Since then, several great racing teams have been based there. Many great drivers have come from the United Kingdom too. It has produced 20 world champions, more than any other nation.

LEWIS HAMILTON 44

PLACE OF BIRTH: *Stevenage, England, United Kingdom*

Sir Lewis Hamilton has at times made racing look easy. However, his road to the top has been anything but smooth. One of the greatest drivers the sport has ever seen has stood out not only for his winning ways but also for his reputation for being unafraid to speak his mind.

Hamilton was eight years old when he started racing in 1993. And he was a winner early and often, tearing through several junior racing levels. Often, Hamilton was the only Black driver where he raced. He often faced discrimination. This would continue to be the case when he joined Formula One in 2007.

In spite of these challenges, he continued to reach podiums at racing's top level. In his first season, he set records for most race wins, pole positions, and points scored by a rookie. He also finished second in the overall standings.

Hamilton won his first title in dramatic fashion the next year. Heading into the final race of the season, Hamilton and Felipe Massa were close in the standings. Massa won the race. That meant Hamilton needed to finish fifth or higher to claim the title. It came down to the final lap. That was when he passed another driver to claim fifth place and the season win. With the victory, the 23-year-old Hamilton became the youngest driver ever to win the World Championship.

It took until 2014 for Hamilton to win another season title. That began a run of six championships in seven years. The one year he didn't win, he finished second. Along the way he became the first driver to reach 100 wins and pole positions and tied Michael Schumacher for most world titles with seven.

ARISE, SIR KNIGHT

Lewis Hamilton was knighted in 2021. In doing so, he became just the fourth Grand Prix racer to receive that honor. He was the first to receive it while still active in the sport.

Lando Norris holds up his trophy after finishing third at the 2022 Emilia Romagna Grand Prix in Imola, Italy.

LANDO NORRIS 4

PLACE OF BIRTH: *Bristol, England, United Kingdom*

Lando Norris set the bar extremely high at an early age. When he was 14 years old, he won the Karting World Championship. No one had won it at a younger age. Norris broke the record set by

Lewis Hamilton. Norris continued to have success as he moved through the junior levels. By 2019 he was ready for a Formula One call-up with McLaren.

In addition to racing talent, Norris might be the most creative driver in Formula One. He designs and paints his own race gear as a hobby.

GEORGE RUSSELL 63

PLACE OF BIRTH: *King's Lynn, England, United Kingdom*

George Russell got the call-up to Formula One in 2019, signing with Williams. While he didn't win as many races as he wanted, he was credited for racing better than his equipment should have allowed him to.

In 2020 he replaced an ill Lewis Hamilton on the Mercedes team for the race in Sakhir, Bahrain. Russell was in the running to win. Unfortunately, a

George Russell's intense style on the track earned him the nickname "Russell the Rocket."

troubled pit stop and bad luck with the car's tires kept him from taking the title. It was still a glimpse of his potential.

In 2022 Mercedes signed him as a full-time driver, making him a teammate of Hamilton's. Russell won his first race that November in Brazil.

Though born in Belgium, Verstappen races under the flag of the Netherlands to honor his father, Jos.

CHAPTER TWO

ON THE CONTINENT

The United Kingdom isn't the only European nation with an impressive Formula One tradition. Several countries on the continent's mainland have their own storied racing pasts. Some of the sport's top drivers form an important part of their countries' cultures.

MAX VERSTAPPEN 1
PLACE OF BIRTH: *Hasselt, Belgium*

Racing is in Max Verstappen's blood. His Dutch father, Jos, was a Formula One driver. His mom, Sophie Kumpen, was a Belgian kart champion.

With that pedigree, it isn't surprising that Max became the youngest competitor in Formula One history in 2015 when he ran his first race at age 17. In 2016 he won his first race at the age of 18 years, 228 days. That triumph made him the youngest race winner in Formula One history.

Verstappen finished in the top four of the final standings every year from 2018 to 2020. In 2021 he became world champion for the first time in his career. The 2021 championship was an epic battle with Lewis Hamilton, and it came down to the final lap of the final race at the Abu Dhabi Grand Prix in the United Arab Emirates. Verstappen was able to overtake Hamilton to win the race and the title.

Verstappen defends his position on the track hard and has an aggressive attitude. This has led to some conflict with fellow racers and even his own team members. But his confidence and

Max Verstappen celebrates on top of his car after winning the 2022 Japanese Grand Prix. The victory also clinched his second straight drivers' championship.

energy have also made him popular with fans over the years. It also helped him dominate his competition. In 2022 Verstappen clinched the title with an incredible four races left in the season. That year he won a record 15 times.

Sebastian Vettel finished his career with 57 pole positions and 53 Grand Prix victories.

SEBASTIAN VETTEL 5

PLACE OF BIRTH: *Heppenheim, Germany*

Sebastian Vettel retired from Formula One racing in 2022, but he left quite a legacy behind. Vettel made his Formula One debut in 2007. A year later, at age 21, he became the youngest Formula One race winner at the time with a victory at the Italian Grand Prix.

In 2010 the 23-year-old became the youngest world champion of all time, breaking the record set by Lewis Hamilton in 2008. That title started a string of four straight Formula One world championships. Vettel's run ended in 2014 when Hamilton took the title. With the pair dominating Formula One, the 2010s saw an intense on-track rivalry between the two great racers. Hamilton later called the battles he experienced with Vettel his favorite.

MICHAEL SCHUMACHER

German-born racer Michael Schumacher retired in 2012 as the greatest champion the sport had seen. When he left racing, he had seven world titles, 91 Grand Prix wins, 155 podium finishes, and 68 pole positions. He had also recorded 77 fastest laps, meaning he was the racer who recorded the fastest individual lap in any race. The superstar spent a record 5,111 total laps in the lead during his career. Lewis Hamilton has since passed or tied most of his records, but Schumacher remains a legend of the sport.

Prior to his retirement, Vettel became an advocate for environmental issues. One of his projects was finding ways to include greener technology within Formula One.

CHARLES LECLERC 16

PLACE OF BIRTH: *Monte Carlo, Monaco*

Charles Leclerc came into Formula One in 2018 with lofty expectations, thanks to a long history of winning. After a successful karting

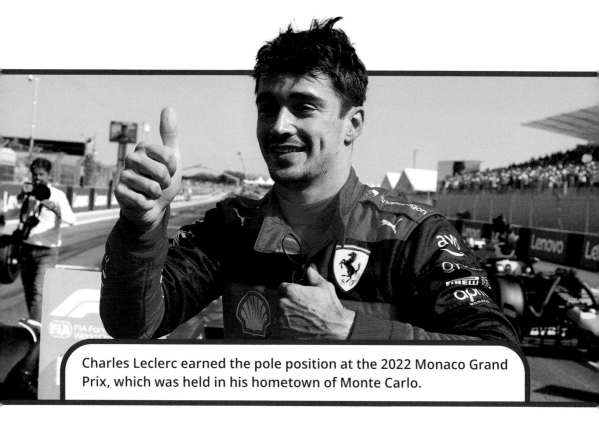

Charles Leclerc earned the pole position at the 2022 Monaco Grand Prix, which was held in his hometown of Monte Carlo.

career, he moved up to open-wheel racing in 2014. Leclerc won back-to-back championships in two different junior levels in 2016 and 2017. He arrived in Formula One in 2018 with a reputation as an aggressive, sometimes reckless driver. During his time at the top level, he has continued to take big chances.

Leclerc signed with Ferrari in 2019. His teammate there was Sebastian Vettel. That year

Leclerc became the first person to outscore Vettel over a season in the team's famous Scuderia model race car, showing that those high expectations could be met.

CARLOS SAINZ JR. 55

PLACE OF BIRTH: *Madrid, Spain*

Carlos Sainz Jr. followed in the footsteps of greatness. His father was a two-time World Rally Champion in the 1990s. Sainz replaced his childhood idol, Fernando Alonso, at McLaren in 2019 and then took the former seat of Sebastian Vettel on the Ferrari team in 2021.

Sainz has also shown he's more than just a driver on his team. He has assisted the team engineers with developing the cars he races in. That expertise helped Sainz claim his first Formula One win at the British Grand Prix in 2022.

Carlos Sainz Jr. holds up his trophy after winning the 2022 British Grand Prix.

Sergio Pérez became the first Mexican driver to win a Formula One race since 1970 when he finished first at the 2020 Sakhir Grand Prix in Bahrain.

CHAPTER THREE

AROUND THE WORLD

Formula One is popular outside of Europe as well. As long as the sport has existed, some of its best competitors have come from around the globe. That remains true, with racers from almost every continent lining up on the starting grid each race day.

SERGIO PÉREZ 11

PLACE OF BIRTH: *Guadalajara, Mexico*

Sergio "Checo" Pérez began his journey to Formula One at the age of six, racing karts in his native Mexico. To make the next step in his career, he

Pérez, *left*, and teammate Max Verstappen, *right*, combined to give Red Bull its first Constructors' Championship in nine years during the 2022 season.

moved to Europe to test his abilities in the highly competitive junior levels.

The move paid off, and he made the leap to Formula One in 2011. There he developed a reputation as a tactical driver who could manage his tires and overcome any disadvantage his equipment might throw at him.

After the 2020 season, he signed with Red Bull and became teammates with Max Verstappen. In the final race of 2021, Pérez's defensive driving helped Verstappen claim his first world title. Pérez helped hold off the charges of Lewis Hamilton.

Pérez has also won plenty of races and has the most career points of any Mexican Formula One driver. Many people call him by his nickname of "Checo," which is what many people in Mexico named Sergio are called.

JUAN MANUEL FANGIO

Argentinian Juan Manuel Fangio is known as the first great champion of Formula One racing. His charm won people over, his showmanship won over crowds, and his tenacity and skill won races. The pioneer of the crowd-pleasing four-wheel drift won five World Championships in six years from 1951 to 1957. And that was despite a severe injury that cost him an entire season. "El Chueco" is still considered by many the finest driver of all time.

Daniel Ricciardo finished the 2022 season with three career wins and eight podium finishes.

DANIEL RICCIARDO ③

PLACE OF BIRTH: *Perth, Australia*

Daniel Ricciardo calls himself "Honey Badger." Outwardly he's laid back and fun. Inside, he's feisty. That spirit led to a lot of success with Red Bull from 2014 through 2018. He then broke two long droughts for new teams. He moved to Renault and in 2020 got the team its first podium finish in nine years. In 2021 he moved to McLaren and got that team's first Grand Prix win since 2012.

Ricciardo's sense of humor is on display with his victory celebration. Known as "the Shoey," he takes a drink from his used, and often sweaty, racing boot.

YUKI TSUNODA 22

PLACE OF BIRTH: *Sagamihara, Japan*

Yuki Tsunoda won often as a kart racer in his native Japan from 2009 to 2016. Once he switched to open-wheel racing, his rise to the top was almost as fast as his lap times. He moved up to Formula One in 2021. That year he was the youngest driver on the track.

Tsunoda became just the 18th Japanese driver to race in Formula One. But his arrival in Formula One has given Japanese fans hope for a future champion from the island nation.

Yuki Tsunoda prepares to run a practice lap at the 2022 Grand Prix of Italy.

Zhou Guanyu chose 24 as his race number to honor American basketball legend Kobe Bryant.

ZHOU GUANYU (24)

PLACE OF BIRTH: *Shanghai, China*

After attending a race at the age of five, Zhou Guanyu knew he wanted to be a Formula One racer. But there had never been a Formula One driver born in China. Zhou wouldn't let that stop him and moved to England when he was 12 to chase his dream. In 2022 he joined Alfa Romeo and became a trailblazer for drivers in his native country.

GLOSSARY

advocate
A person who supports or promotes the interests of a cause or group.

drift
A controlled slide in a race car caused by oversteering the car around a corner.

karting
Road racing done in smaller vehicles commonly known as go-karts.

knighted
To be given the honor of knighthood by the royal family of the United Kingdom; the honor is given to someone doing impactful work in his profession.

open-wheel racing
Racing done in cars where the wheels are outside the vehicle's main body.

pedigree
A distinguished family line or history.

podium
A platform that holds the top three finishers of a race.

pole position
The most favorable position at the start of an auto race, typically in the inside of the front row.

tactical
Referring to carefully planned actions or strategy.

MORE INFORMATION

BOOKS

Hewson, Anthony K. *The Best Moments in Formula One*. Minneapolis, MN: Abdo Publishing, 2024.

Hustad, Douglas. *Innovations in Auto Racing*. Minneapolis, MN: Abdo Publishing, 2022.

Rule, Heather. *GOATs of Auto Racing*. Minneapolis, MN: Abdo Publishing, 2022.

ONLINE RESOURCES

To learn more about the best drivers of Formula One, please visit **abdobooklinks.com** or scan this QR code. These links are routinely monitored and updated to provide the most current information available.

INDEX

ABOUT THE AUTHOR

Corbu Stathes grew up loving all things sports and continues to work in the field to this day. He first learned about the joys of going fast on his bike and then in a revved-up golf cart. Today he obeys all traffic laws, including the speed limit. He lives in Minnesota with his son.